Prompt Engineering ; The Future Of Language Generation

Michael Ferguson

Published by Michael Ferguson, 2023.

While every precaution has been taken in the preparation of this book, the publisher assumes no responsibility for errors or omissions, or for damages resulting from the use of the information contained herein.

PROMPT ENGINEERING ; THE FUTURE OF LANGUAGE GENERATION

First edition. January 27, 2023.

ISBN: 979-8215905739

Written by Michael Ferguson.

"To the trailblazers in the field of AI-powered language generation, who have pushed the boundaries of what is possible and continue to inspire us to innovate. To the dedicated developers, researchers, and engineers who work tirelessly to create intelligent conversational systems that improve our daily lives. And to the future generation of AI prompt engineers, who will take the field to new heights. This book is dedicated to you all."

AI Prompt Engineering: The Future of Language Generation

By: Michael C. Ferguson

"AI Prompt Engineering: The Future of Language Generation" is a comprehensive guide to the cutting-edge field of AI-powered language generation. Written with the help and knowledge of experts in the field, this book covers everything from the basics of AI prompt engineering to advanced techniques and best practices for building intelligent chatbots and other conversational systems.

The book begins by introducing the reader to the fundamental concepts and technologies that underpin AI prompt engineering, such as natural language processing (NLP) and machine learning (ML). It then delves into the specific techniques and tools used in the development of AI-powered language generation systems, including neural networks, deep learning, and reinforcement learning.

Throughout the book, we will provide practical examples and case studies that demonstrate how these techniques can be applied in real-world scenarios. They also discuss the ethical and social implications of AI-powered language generation and explore the future possibilities of this rapidly advancing field.

Without a doubt, "AI Prompt Engineering: The Future of Language Generation" is an essential resource for anyone interested in the development and application of AI-powered language generation technology. Whether you are a developer, a researcher, or simply someone with a passion for technology, this book will provide you with a deep understanding of the field and help you stay ahead of the curve in the world of AI prompt engineering.

Table of Contents:

- The impact of AI-generated language on human communication

Chapter 6: The Future of AI Prompt Engineering

- Advancements in technology and techniques
- Emerging applications and use cases
- Challenges and opportunities for the field

Chapter 7: Conclusion and Resources

- Summary of key takeaways
- Suggestions for further reading and resources
- Conclusion on the future of AI prompt engineering
- References and Bibliography

Chapter 1: Introduction to AI Prompt Engineering

Artificial intelligence (AI) has been one of the most transformative technologies of the 21st century, with applications in a wide range of fields including healthcare, finance, transportation, and entertainment. One of the most promising areas of AI research is AI-powered language generation, also known as AI prompt engineering.

AI prompt engineering is the process of using artificial intelligence to generate human-like language. This technology has the potential to revolutionize how we interact with machines, enabling more natural and intuitive communication between humans and computers.

In this chapter, we will provide an overview of AI prompt engineering and its applications. We will also cover the fundamentals of natural language processing (NLP) and machine learning (ML), which are the two key technologies that underpin AI-powered language generation. Finally, we will discuss the historical developments and current state of the field, highlighting some of the major milestones and breakthroughs in AI prompt engineering.

The field of AI prompt engineering is an interdisciplinary one, drawing on expertise from computer science, linguistics, cognitive science, and other fields. NLP is the branch of AI and computer science concerned with the interactions between computers and human languages, and it is a crucial component of AI-powered language generation. ML, on the other hand, is a method of teaching computers to learn from data, and it is used to train AI models to generate human-like language.

One of the most prominent applications of AI prompt engineering is in building chatbots, which are computer programs that are designed to simulate conversation with human users. Chatbots have been used in a variety of contexts, from customer service to entertainment. Another application of AI prompt engineering is in creating AI-generated text, such as automated news articles, social media posts, and even poetry.

In recent years, the field of AI prompt engineering has seen significant advancements thanks to advances in deep learning and neural networks. These technologies have enabled the development of more sophisticated and human-like language generation systems. However, there are still many challenges to be addressed, including issues related to bias, privacy, and the impact of AI-generated language on human communication.

Overall, AI prompt engineering is a rapidly advancing field with enormous potential for shaping the way we interact with machines and each other. This book will provide an in-depth examination of the field, covering everything from the basics of AI prompt engineering to advanced techniques and best practices for building intelligent chatbots and other conversational systems.We will also delve deeper into the specific techniques and tools used in the development of AI-powered language generation systems. We will cover the following topics:

- Neural networks and deep learning
- Reinforcement learning
- Transfer learning and pre-training
- Evaluation and optimization techniques

Neural networks are a type of machine learning model that is inspired by the structure of the human brain. They consist of layers of interconnected "neurons" that process and transmit information. Deep learning is a subfield of machine learning that is based on neural networks and is used to train models with many layers, or "deep" neural networks. Deep learning has been used to achieve state-of-the-art performance in a wide range of applications, including image recognition, natural language processing, and speech recognition.

Reinforcement learning is another type of machine learning that is based on the idea of training an agent to take actions in an environment to maximize a reward. This is a useful technique for training chatbots and other conversational systems, as it allows the agent to learn from its interactions with users.

Transfer learning and pre-training are techniques that can be used to improve the performance of AI models by leveraging knowledge from related tasks. In the case of AI-powered language generation, transfer learning can be used to transfer knowledge from pre-trained models to new tasks, while pre-training can be used to train models on large amounts of data before fine-tuning them on smaller, task-specific datasets.

Finally, we will discuss evaluation and optimization techniques that can be used to measure the performance of AI-powered language generation systems and improve their quality. This includes metrics for evaluating the quality of generated text, such as perplexity, BLEU score, ROUGE and others. We will also cover techniques for optimizing the parameters of AI models, such as gradient descent and backpropagation.

By the end of this chapter, readers will have a solid understanding of the techniques and tools used in the development of AI-powered language generation systems and will be equipped with the knowledge needed to build their own conversational systems.

Chapter 1: Part 1: Overview of AI prompt engineering

AI prompt engineering is the process of using artificial intelligence to generate human-like language. This technology has the potential to revolutionize how we interact with machines, enabling more natural and intuitive communication between humans and computers.

One of the most prominent applications of AI prompt engineering is in building chatbots, which are computer programs that are designed to simulate conversation with human users. Chatbots have been used in a variety of contexts, from customer service to entertainment. Another application of AI prompt engineering is in creating AI-generated text, such as automated news articles, social media posts, and even poetry.

AI-generated text can be used to automate repetitive tasks, such as writing reports, articles or even composing emails, it can also be used in creative writing, such as poetry, lyrics, or fiction. In addition, AI-generated text can be used to augment human capabilities, like adding captions or subtitles to videos, creating content for social media, or even creating chatbot responses.

AI prompt engineering also has the potential to improve accessibility by providing support for people with disabilities, such as creating text-to-speech systems, or speech-to-text systems, which can help people with visual or auditory impairments.

With that said, AI prompt engineering is a rapidly advancing field with enormous potential for shaping the way we interact with machines and each other. This field draws on expertise from computer science, linguistics, cognitive science, and other fields to create more natural and intuitive ways of communicating with computers.

PROMPT ENGINEERING ; THE FUTURE OF LANGUAGE GENERATION

Deeper in the chapter you will find an overview of AI prompt engineering and its applications, covering the basics of the field and highlighting some of the most exciting possibilities for the future of AI-powered language generation.

Chapter 1 Part 2 - Fundamentals of natural language processing and machine learning

As mentioned earlier, the field of AI prompt engineering is an interdisciplinary one, drawing on expertise from computer science, linguistics, cognitive science, and other fields. Two key technologies that underpin AI-powered language generation are natural language processing (NLP) and machine learning (ML).

Natural language processing (NLP) is the branch of AI and computer science concerned with the interactions between computers and human languages. NLP is a complex field that involves many different sub-disciplines, such as syntactic analysis, semantic analysis, and pragmatics.

One of the main challenges in NLP is dealing with the complexity and ambiguity of human language. For example, words can have multiple meanings depending on the context in which they are used, and sentences can have multiple interpretations. NLP techniques such as Part-of-Speech Tagging, Named Entity Recognition, and Dependency Parsing, among others, can be used to extract meaning from text, and then the information can be used to train machine learning models.

Machine learning (ML) is a method of teaching computers to learn from data. ML is used to train AI models to generate human-like language. There are different types of machine learning, including supervised learning, unsupervised learning, and reinforcement learning.

Supervised learning is used to train models on labeled data, where the correct output is known. For example, supervised learning can be used to train a model to generate text by providing it with a large dataset of text and the corresponding output.

Unsupervised learning, on the other hand, is used to find patterns in data without any labeled output. This can be useful for tasks such as language translation or text summarization.

Reinforcement learning is a type of machine learning that is based on the idea of training an agent to take actions in an environment to maximize a reward. This is a useful technique for training chatbots and other conversational systems, as it allows the agent to learn from its interactions with users.

By the end of this chapter, readers will have a good understanding of the fundamentals of natural language processing and machine learning, and how these technologies are used in the development of AI-powered language generation systems.

In addition to these basic techniques, there are also more advanced methods that can be used to improve the performance of AI-powered language generation systems. One of these is deep learning, which is a subfield of machine learning that is based on neural networks and is used to train models with many layers, or "deep" neural networks. Deep learning has been used to achieve state-of-the-art performance in a wide range of applications, including image recognition, natural language processing, and speech recognition.

Another advanced technique is transfer learning, which is a method of using knowledge from a pre-trained model to improve the performance of a new model. This can be useful for tasks such as language generation, where it can be difficult to obtain large amounts of labeled data. By using transfer learning, a model can be pre-trained on a large dataset of text, and then fine-tuned on a smaller dataset of text for a specific task.

Furthermore, pre-training is another technique that can be used to improve the performance of AI-powered language generation systems. Pre-training refers to training a model on a large dataset of text or other data before fine-tuning it on a smaller dataset for a specific task. This can be useful for tasks such as language generation, where it can be difficult to obtain large amounts of labeled data.

Evaluation and optimization techniques are also important in AI prompt engineering. These techniques are used to measure the performance of AI-powered language generation systems and improve their quality. Metrics like perplexity, BLEU score, ROUGE and others can be used to evaluate the quality of generated text. And techniques like gradient descent and backpropagation can be used to optimize the parameters of AI models.

In summary, AI prompt engineering draws on a range of techniques from natural language processing and machine learning, from the basics to the more advanced methods, to create more natural and intuitive ways of communicating with computers. In the following chapters, we will delve deeper into these techniques and explore how they can be applied in real-world scenarios.

Chapter 1 Part 3: Historical developments and current state of the field

The field of AI prompt engineering has a long history, dating back to the early days of computer science. Some of the earliest efforts to generate human-like language using computers can be traced back to the 1950s and 1960s, when researchers began experimenting with rule-based systems for language generation. These systems relied on a set of pre-defined rules to generate text, and while they were able to produce simple responses, they were limited in their ability to understand and generate more complex language.

In the 1970s and 1980s, researchers began to explore the use of statistical methods for language generation. These methods relied on probability models to generate text, and they proved to be more effective than rule-based systems. However, they still had limitations and were not able to generate text that was indistinguishable from human-generated text.

The field of AI prompt engineering began to take off in the 1990s and 2000s, with the advent of machine learning and deep learning. These technologies made it possible to train AI models on large amounts of data, and they have been used to achieve significant improvements in the quality of AI-generated text.

One of the most significant breakthroughs in the field came in the form of recurrent neural networks (RNNs), which are a type of neural network that are well-suited to sequence data, like text. RNNs, and their variants like LSTM and GRU, made it possible to generate text that was more coherent and human-like than ever before.

In recent years, the field of AI prompt engineering has seen even more rapid advances, thanks to the development of large-scale pre-training models like GPT and BERT, these models were trained on a massive amount of data and can generate text that is highly coherent, and in some cases, it is difficult to distinguish between the text generated by the models and text written by humans.

In the current state of the field, AI prompt engineering is being applied in a wide range of industries and applications, from customer service and e-commerce to entertainment and media. For example, OpenAI's GPT-3 has been used to create chatbots and virtual assistants, generate automated news articles, and even compose poetry. Other companies like HuggingFace, have developed models like DialoGPT, that are specialized in generating human-like dialogue and are being used in chatbots and virtual assistants.

In the field of entertainment, AI-generated text is being used to create interactive stories and games, as well as to generate lyrics and music. In the field of education, AI-generated text is being used to create personalized learning materials and assessments, and in the field of healthcare, AI-generated text is being used to create patient records and generate diagnostic reports.

In addition to these examples, AI prompt engineering is also being applied in other areas such as finance, transportation, and smart home systems. In finance, AI-generated text can be used to create financial reports and predictions, in transportation, AI-generated text can be used to generate traffic updates and navigation instructions, and in smart home systems, AI-generated text can be used to control devices and provide information to users.

Despite these advancements, there are still many challenges to be addressed in the field of AI prompt engineering. One of the main challenges is dealing with the complexity and ambiguity of human language. The field of AI prompt engineering is also facing ethical and social implications, such as privacy and security concerns, bias and fairness in AI-generated language, and the impact of AI-generated language on human communication.

Overall, the field of AI prompt engineering is constantly evolving and advancing, with new breakthroughs and developments happening all the time. This field has the potential to revolutionize the way we interact with machines, and it will be exciting to see how it continues to shape the future.

In the following chapters, we will explore the practical applications of AI prompt engineering and the ethical and social implications that come with it. We will also look at the future possibilities of this rapidly advancing field.

Chapter 2: Techniques and Tools for AI Prompt Engineering

This chapter covers the specific techniques and tools used in the development of AI-powered language generation systems. The chapter covers the following topics:

- Neural networks and deep learning
- Reinforcement learning
- Transfer learning and pre-training
- Evaluation and optimization techniques

The chapter begins by explaining the concept of Neural networks, a type of machine learning model that is inspired by the structure of the human brain. They consist of layers of interconnected "neurons" that process and transmit information. The chapter also covers deep learning, a subfield of machine learning that is based on neural networks and is used to train models with many layers, or "deep" neural networks. Deep learning has been used to achieve state-of-the-art performance in a wide range of applications, including image recognition, natural language processing, and speech recognition.

The chapter then goes on to explain the concept of Reinforcement learning, another type of machine learning that is based on the idea of training an agent to take actions in an environment in order to maximize a reward. This is a useful technique for training chatbots and other conversational systems, as it allows the agent to learn from its interactions with users.

The chapter also covers Transfer learning and pre-training, which are techniques that can be used to improve the performance of AI models by leveraging knowledge from related tasks. In the case of AI-powered language generation, transfer learning can be used to transfer knowledge from pre-trained models to new tasks, while pre-training can be used to train models on large amounts of data before fine-tuning them on smaller, task-specific datasets.

Finally, the chapter covers Evaluation and optimization techniques that can be used to measure the performance of AI-powered language generation systems and improve their quality. This includes metrics for evaluating the quality of generated text, such as perplex

Chapter 2 Part 1: Neural Networks And Deep Learning

Neural networks are a type of machine learning model that is inspired by the structure of the human brain. They consist of layers of interconnected "neurons" that process and transmit information. Neural networks are trained by adjusting the weights of the connections between the neurons in order to minimize the error between the predicted output and the actual output.

Deep learning is a subfield of machine learning that is based on neural networks and is used to train models with many layers, or "deep" neural networks. Deep learning has been used to achieve state-of-the-art performance in a wide range of applications, including image recognition, natural language processing, and speech recognition.

One of the most popular neural network architectures used in deep learning is the feedforward neural network, which consists of an input layer, one or more hidden layers, and an output layer. The input layer receives the input data, and the output layer produces the predicted output. The hidden layers are used to process the data and extract features that are used to make the prediction.

Another popular neural network architecture is the recurrent neural network (RNN), which is well-suited to sequence data, like text. RNNs can be used to generate text by using the previous words in a sentence to predict the next word. RNNs are also used in other tasks such as language translation, text summarization and speech recognition.

One of the most advanced variants of RNNs are LSTM (Long Short-Term Memory) and GRU (Gated Recurrent Unit), these architectures are designed to improve the performance of RNNs by addressing the problem of vanishing gradients, which occurs when the information flows through multiple layers in the network. LSTM and GRU networks introduce "memory cells" that can store information for longer periods of time, allowing the network to make predictions based on more context. These architectures have been used to achieve state-of-the-art performance in many natural language processing tasks such as language generation and language translation.

Convolutional neural networks (CNNs) are another type of neural network architecture that is commonly used in deep learning. CNNs are particularly well-suited for image and video recognition tasks because they are able to extract features from images and videos by applying convolutions to the data.

There are also other architectures such as Transformer networks that have been developed recently, they are based on the attention mechanism, which allows the model to weigh different parts of the input when making a prediction. Transformer networks have been used to achieve state-of-the-art performance in a wide range of natural language processing tasks, such as language generation and language translation.

In summary, neural networks and deep learning are powerful techniques that are widely used in the development of AI-powered language generation systems. These techniques allow us to train models that can extract features from large amounts of data and generate human-like text. The variety of architectures available allows for a range of different tasks to be performed, and the advancements in architectures like LSTM, GRU, CNN and Transformer networks have led to substantial improvements in the quality of AI-generated text.

Chapter 2 Part 2: Reinforcement Learning

Reinforcement learning (RL) is a type of machine learning that is based on the idea of training an agent to take actions in an environment in order to maximize a reward. In the context of AI prompt engineering, RL can be used to train chatbots and other conversational systems by allowing the agent to learn from its interactions with users.

In RL, an agent interacts with an environment, and at each time step, the agent selects an action based on its current state. After the action is taken, the environment provides the agent with a reward and the agent's state changes. The agent's goal is to learn a policy, which is a mapping from states to actions, that maximizes the expected cumulative reward over time.

One of the most popular RL algorithms is Q-learning, which is an off-policy algorithm that can be used to learn a policy for a deterministic environment. Q-learning is based on the idea of estimating the value of each state-action pair, and the agent selects the action that has the highest value.

Another popular RL algorithm is SARSA, which is an on-policy algorithm that can be used to learn a policy for a stochastic environment. SARSA is based on the idea of estimating the value of each state-action pair, and the agent selects the action that has the highest value based on the current state and the current policy.

There are also other RL algorithms such as Actor-Critic, A3C, PPO, and DDPG that have been developed recently and have been used to train agents for a variety of tasks, including chatbot and other conversational systems.

In addition, RL is being combined with other techniques such as Deep Learning and pre-training to improve the performance of AI-powered language generation systems, this is called Deep Reinforcement Learning.

In summary, reinforcement learning is a powerful technique that can be used to train chatbots and other conversational systems. RL algorithms such as Q-learning, SARSA and other recent developments allow for the agent to learn from its interactions with users and improve its performance over time. The combination of RL with other techniques such as deep learning and pre-training can lead to even better performance.

When training an agent using RL, it's important to define the reward function, which is a function that assigns a scalar value to each state-action pair. The reward function is used to guide the agent's learning process and it should be designed to reflect the desired behavior of the agent.

In the case of chatbots and other conversational systems, the reward function can be based on metrics such as task completion rate, user satisfaction, and conversation length. For example, the agent can be given a positive reward for successfully completing a task, a negative reward for an unsatisfied user, and a neutral reward for an average conversation length.

Another important aspect of RL is the exploration-exploitation trade-off, which refers to the balance between exploring new actions and exploiting the actions that have been learned so far. The agent needs to explore new actions in order to learn a good policy, but at the same time, it needs to exploit the actions that it has learned so far in order to maximize the reward.

There are different techniques that can be used to balance exploration and exploitation, such as epsilon-greedy, which is a simple technique that adds a probability of choosing a random action rather than the action with the highest value, and Thompson sampling, which is a more advanced technique that samples actions based on the uncertainty of the estimates.

One of the main challenges of RL is dealing with the high dimensionality and complexity of the state space. The state space of a chatbot or conversational system can be very large, making it difficult for the agent to learn a good policy. One way to address this challenge is by using function approximation, which is a technique that allows the agent to approximate the value of states that it has not seen before.

Another way to address this challenge is by using a combination of RL and other techniques such as deep learning and pre-training. This can help to improve the performance of the agent by leveraging prior knowledge and reducing the dimensionality of the state space.

In conclusion, RL is a powerful technique that can be used to train chatbots and other conversational systems. It allows the agent to learn from its interactions with users and improve its performance over time. However, it also poses some challenges such as defining the reward function, balancing exploration and exploitation, and dealing with the high dimensionality and complexity of the state space. These challenges can be addressed by using techniques such as function approximation and by combining RL with other techniques such as deep learning and pre-training.

It's worth noting that, while RL can be a powerful tool for training chatbots and conversational systems, it's not always the best approach and it depends on the specific use case. For example, if the task is well-defined and the goal is to follow a set of predefined rules, a rule-based approach may be more suitable. However, if the task is more open-ended and the goal is to improve the agent's performance over time, RL can be a powerful tool.

PROMPT ENGINEERING ; THE FUTURE OF LANGUAGE GENERATION

In the following sections of the book, we will delve deeper into the specific techniques and tools used in AI prompt engineering and explore how they can be applied in real-world scenarios.

Chapter 2 part 3: Transfer learning and pre-training

Transfer learning and pre-training are techniques that can be used to improve the performance of AI models by leveraging knowledge from related tasks. In the context of AI prompt engineering, these techniques can be used to train models that generate human-like text.

Transfer learning is the process of using a pre-trained model as a starting point for a new task. This can be useful when the new task has limited data or resources, as the pre-trained model can provide a good initialization for the new task. The pre-trained model can also be fine-tuned on the new task, by adjusting the weights of the model to fit the new data.

Pre-training is the process of training a model on a large amount of data before fine-tuning it on a smaller, task-specific dataset. This can be useful when the task-specific dataset is small or when the model needs to be able to generalize to new data.

One of the most popular pre-training techniques is unsupervised pre-training, which is the process of training a model on a large amount of unannotated data. This can be useful for tasks such as language generation, where the model can learn to generate text that is similar to the text in the unannotated data.

Another popular pre-training technique is self-supervised pre-training, which is the process of training a model on a large amount of data that has been annotated with a weak supervision signal. This can be useful for tasks such as language understanding, where the model can learn to understand the meaning of the text.

PROMPT ENGINEERING ; THE FUTURE OF LANGUAGE GENERATION

Large-scale pre-training models like GPT-3 and BERT, have been trained on massive amounts of data and can generate text that is highly coherent, and in some cases, it is difficult to distinguish between the text generated by the models and text written by humans.

Pre-training and transfer learning can be used together to improve the performance of AI-powered language generation systems, by leveraging prior knowledge from related tasks and fine-tuning the model to fit the specific task.

In the next sections, we will explore how pre-training and transfer learning can be used in real-world scenarios and their specific applications in different industries.

In addition, pre-training and transfer learning can also be used in combination with other techniques such as neural networks and deep learning, to further improve the performance of AI-powered language generation systems. For example, a pre-trained model can be fine-tuned using a deep learning architecture, such as a LSTM or a Transformer network, to perform a specific task.

One important aspect of pre-training and transfer learning is the choice of the pre-training dataset. The pre-training data set should be large and diverse, in order to provide the model with a broad range of knowledge. The pre-training dataset should also be relevant to the task-specific dataset, in order to ensure that the model can generalize well to the new data.

Another important aspect is the fine-tuning process, which is the process of adjusting the weights of the pre-trained model to fit the new task. The fine-tuning process should be done carefully, in order to avoid overfitting and to ensure that the model can generalize well to new data.

Overall, pre-training and transfer learning are powerful techniques that can be used to improve the performance of AI-powered language generation systems. These techniques allow us to leverage prior knowledge from related tasks and to train models that can generate human-like text with high coherence and relevance.

It's worth mentioning that these techniques are not only applied to natural language processing but also to other fields such as computer vision and speech recognition, where pre-training and transfer learning have been widely used to improve the performance of AI models.

Chapter 2 Part 4: Evaluation and optimization techniques

Evaluation and optimization techniques are important tools that can be used to measure the performance of AI-powered language generation systems and improve their quality. These techniques are essential to ensure that the generated text is coherent, relevant and human-like.

One commonly used evaluation technique is perplexity, which is a measure of how well a probability distribution predicts a given set of data. Lower perplexity values indicate that the model's predictions are more likely, and therefore the generated text is more coherent and relevant.

Another commonly used evaluation technique is BLEU, which is a measure of the similarity between the generated text and a reference text. BLEU scores range from 0 to 1, with 1 indicating that the generated text is identical to the reference text.

Another evaluation technique is METEOR, which is a measure of the similarity between the generated text and a reference text that takes into account synonyms, stemming, and paraphrasing. METEOR scores range from 0 to 1, with 1 indicating that the generated text is identical to the reference text.

Another evaluation technique is ROUGE, which is a measure of the similarity between the generated text and a reference text based on n-gram overlap. ROUGE scores range from 0 to 1, with 1 indicating that the generated text is identical to the reference text.

In addition to these evaluation techniques, there are also human evaluation methods that involve having human evaluators rate the quality of the generated text. These methods can provide more accurate and detailed feedback on the performance of the model, but they are also more time-consuming and costly.

Once the performance of the AI-powered language generation system has been evaluated, optimization techniques can be used to improve the quality of the generated text. These techniques include adjusting the model's architecture, fine-tuning the model's hyperparameters, and using techniques such as regularization and early stopping to prevent overfitting.

Another optimization technique is data augmentation, which is the process of generating new data by applying various transformations to the existing data. This can be useful for tasks such as language generation, where the model can learn to generate text that is similar to augmented data.

Another optimization technique is curriculum learning, which is the process of training a model on a sequence of tasks, where each task is designed to be more challenging than the previous one. This can be useful for tasks such as language understanding, where the model can learn to understand the meaning of text in a progressive manner.

One of the most important optimization techniques is active learning, which is the process of selecting the most informative data samples to train the model on. This can be useful for tasks such as language generation, where the model can learn to generate text that is similar to the selected data samples.

In summary, evaluation and optimization techniques are essential tools that can be used to measure the performance of AI-powered language generation systems and improve their quality. These techniques include using metrics such as perplexity, BLEU and METEOR, human evaluation methods, and techniques such as data augmentation, curriculum learning, and active learning.

PROMPT ENGINEERING ; THE FUTURE OF LANGUAGE GENERATION

It's worth mentioning that evaluating and optimizing AI models is an ongoing process that requires iteration and continuous monitoring, as the model's performance may change over time due to changes in the data distribution.

Chapter 3: Building Intelligent Chatbots

This chapter of the book focuses on building intelligent chatbots. A chatbot is a computer program designed to simulate a conversation with human users. They can be used in a variety of applications such as customer service, e-commerce, and entertainment.

The first step in building a chatbot is to define the task and the goals of the chatbot. The task can be something as simple as answering frequently asked questions or providing information about a product or service, or something as complex as conducting a conversation in natural language. The goals of the chatbot can be defined in terms of metrics such as task completion rate, user satisfaction, and conversation length.

Once the task and goals have been defined, the next step is to design the conversational flow of the chatbot. This involves creating a script that defines the possible paths that the conversation can take, and the responses of the chatbot to different user inputs. The script can be designed using flowcharts or other visual tools.

The next step is to implement the chatbot using a programming language such as Python or Java. This involves writing code that implements the conversational flow, and interacts with the user through a user interface such as a web page or mobile app. The chatbot can be implemented using a rule-based approach or a machine learning-based approach.

The rule-based approach involves creating a set of rules that the chatbot follows to determine its responses. This approach is simple and easy to implement, but it can be limited in terms of its ability to understand natural language and to handle variations in the user input.

The machine learning-based approach, on the other hand, involves training a model on a dataset of examples of conversation, and using the trained model to generate responses. This approach can handle variations in the user input and can understand natural language better, but it can require more data and computational resources.

One of the most popular machine learning-based approaches is the use of neural networks, which are a type of model that can be trained to generate text. There are different types of neural networks that can be used, such as Recurrent Neural Networks (RNN) and Transformer networks. These networks can be pre-trained on large amounts of data and fine-tuned on a task-specific dataset.

Another popular approach is the use of reinforcement learning (RL) to train the chatbot. RL allows the chatbot to learn from its interactions with users and improve its performance over time. This can be done by defining a reward function that reflects the desired behavior of the chatbot and training the chatbot to maximize the reward.

Evaluation and optimization techniques are also important when building a chatbot. These techniques can be used to measure the performance of the chatbot and improve its quality. Common evaluation metrics include perplexity, BLEU, and METEOR. Optimization techniques include adjusting the model's architecture, fine-tuning the model's hyperparameters, and using techniques such as data augmentation and active learning.

In conclusion, building an intelligent chatbot involves a series of steps, including defining the task and goals, designing the conversational flow, implementing the chatbot, training the chatbot using machine learning or reinforcement learning, evaluating the performance and optimizing the chatbot. The use of pre-training and transfer learning can also be used to improve the performance of the chatbot.

Chapter 3 Part 1: Designing conversational systems

Designing conversational systems is an important step in building intelligent chatbots. The design of the conversational system involves creating a script that defines the possible paths that the conversation can take, and the responses of the chatbot to different user inputs. The script can be designed using flowcharts or other visual tools.

The first step in designing a conversational system is to understand the user's needs and goals. This involves identifying the user's pain points and the tasks that the chatbot should be able to perform. For example, if the chatbot is designed for customer service, the user's pain points may include long wait times and difficulty finding information. The chatbot's tasks may include answering frequently asked questions and providing information about a product or service.

The next step is to design the conversational flow. This involves creating a script that defines the possible paths that the conversation can take, and the responses of the chatbot to different user inputs. The script can be designed using flowcharts or other visual tools. The flowchart should be clear, easy to follow, and should take into account the user's needs and goals.

It's important to consider the different ways that the user may initiate the conversation, and how the chatbot should respond. For example, the user may start the conversation by asking a question, making a statement, or giving a command. The chatbot should be able to recognize these different types of inputs and respond appropriately.

The chatbot's responses should be clear, concise, and relevant to the user's input. The chatbot should also be able to handle variations in the user's input, such as synonyms and different word forms. It's important to consider the different ways that the user may phrase their input and to design the chatbot's responses accordingly.

The chatbot should also be able to handle errors and unexpected inputs. For example, if the user inputs an invalid command or asks a question that the chatbot is not able to answer, the chatbot should respond with an appropriate message and ask the user to rephrase their input.

It's also important to consider the user's emotional state and to design the chatbot's responses accordingly. For example, if the user is frustrated or angry, the chatbot's responses should be calm and empathetic.

Finally, it's important to test the chatbot's script with users to ensure that it meets their needs and that it is easy to use. This can be done by conducting user testing sessions and gathering feedback from users.

In conclusion, designing a conversational system is an important step in building intelligent chatbots. It involves understanding the user's needs and goals, designing the conversational flow, considering the different ways that the user may initiate the conversation, handling errors and unexpected inputs, and testing the chatbot's script with users.

Chapter 3 – Part 2: Creating Chatbot Personalities

Creating a chatbot personality is an important aspect of designing conversational systems. The chatbot's personality can influence how users perceive the chatbot and their willingness to interact with it. A well-designed personality can make the chatbot more engaging and can improve the user's experience.

One way to create a chatbot personality is to use a pre-defined set of characteristics. For example, the chatbot could be designed to be friendly, helpful, and empathetic. These characteristics can be reflected in the chatbot's tone of voice, the way it responds to user inputs, and the type of language it uses.

Another way to create a chatbot personality is to use machine learning techniques. For example, the chatbot could be trained on a dataset of examples of human conversation, and the personality could be inferred from the data. This can be useful for creating a chatbot that can understand natural language and that can generate text that is similar to human text.

It's important to note that the chatbot's personality should be consistent with the brand and the task that the chatbot is designed to perform. For example, a chatbot that is designed for customer service should have a helpful and empathetic personality, while a chatbot that is designed for entertainment should have a more playful personality.

It's also important to consider the user's emotional state and to adjust the chatbot's personality accordingly. For example, if the user is frustrated or angry, the chatbot's personality should be calm and empathetic.

It's also important to test the chatbot's personality with users to ensure that it meets their needs and that it is easy to use. This can be done by conducting user testing sessions and gathering feedback from users.

Additionally, it's important to consider the cultural and demographic background of the target audience and tailor the chatbot's personality accordingly. For example, if the target audience is primarily from a specific culture, the chatbot's personality should reflect the cultural norms and values of that culture.

Another aspect to consider is the gender of the chatbot, as it may have an impact on the user's perception of the chatbot. For example, a chatbot designed to have a male personality may be perceived differently than a chatbot designed to have a female personality.

In addition, it is also important to consider the ages of the target audience, as different age groups may prefer different types of personalities. For example, older adults may prefer a more formal and polite personality, while younger adults may prefer a more casual and friendly personality.

In conclusion, creating a chatbot personality is an important aspect of designing conversational systems. It can be done by using pre-defined characteristics, machine learning techniques, and by testing the chatbot's personality with users. It's important to keep in mind that the chatbot's personality should be consistent with the brand and the task that the chatbot is designed to perform, and it should be adjusted based on the user's emotional state, cultural and demographic background, gender, and ages of the target audience.

Chapter 3 Part 3: Handling user input and providing context-aware responses

Handling user input and providing context-aware responses are important aspects of designing conversational systems. The chatbot's ability to understand the user's input and respond appropriately can greatly influence the user's experience.

One way to handle user input is to use rule-based systems. This approach involves creating a set of rules that the chatbot follows to determine its responses. The rules can be based on keywords or patterns in the user's input. This approach is simple and easy to implement, but it can be limited in terms of its ability to understand natural language and to handle variations in the user input.

Another way to handle user input is to use machine learning-based approaches. For example, the chatbot could be trained on a dataset of examples of human conversation, and the model can be used to generate responses based on the user's input. This approach can handle variations in the user input and can understand natural language better, but it can require more data and computational resources.

To provide context-aware responses, the chatbot should be able to maintain the context of the conversation. This can be done by keeping track of the previous user inputs and using them to generate responses that are relevant to the current context of the conversation. For example, if the user asked a question about a product, the chatbot should be able to provide relevant information about that product in its response.

One way to provide context-aware responses is to use natural language understanding (NLU) techniques. These techniques can be used to extract entities, intents, and sentiments from the user's input. The extracted information can be used to generate context-aware responses.

Another way to provide context-aware responses is to use dialogue management techniques. These techniques can be used to keep track of the conversation state, and to generate responses that are appropriate for the current conversation state.

Additionally, the chatbot can use a memory network to store information about the conversation and users. This can be used to generate context-aware responses, by providing the chatbot with a history of the conversation.

It is also important to consider the user's emotional state when providing context-aware responses. For example, if the user is frustrated or angry, the chatbot's responses should be calm and empathetic. This can be done by using sentiment analysis techniques to detect the user's emotions and adjusting the chatbot's responses accordingly.

Another important aspect of context-aware responses is to provide personalized responses. For example, if the chatbot has collected information about the user, it can use that information to provide personalized recommendations or information. This can improve the user's experience, as the chatbot will be able to provide more relevant and useful information.

It's also important to test the chatbot's ability to handle user input and provide context-aware responses with users to ensure that it meets their needs and that it is easy to use. This can be done by conducting user testing sessions and gathering feedback from users.

In conclusion, handling user input and providing context-aware responses are important aspects of designing conversational systems. It can be done by using rule-based systems, machine learning techniques, natural language understanding techniques, dialogue management techniques, memory networks, and by testing the chatbot's ability to handle user input and provide context-aware responses with users. It's important to keep in mind that the chatbot should be able to understand the user's input, maintain the context of the conversation, provide personalized and appropriate responses, and take into account the user's emotional state.

Chapter 3 Part 4 – Best Practices for Chatbot Development

Best practices for chatbot development are essential for creating effective and user-friendly conversational systems. These practices can help to ensure that the chatbot meets the needs of the user, is easy to use, and provides a positive experience.

One best practice for chatbot development is to start by defining the task and goals of the chatbot. This involves identifying the user's pain points and the tasks that the chatbot should be able to perform. This helps to ensure that the chatbot is designed to meet the needs of the user and that it is focused on the task at hand.

Another best practice is to design the conversational flow. This involves creating a script that defines the possible paths that the conversation can take, and the responses of the chatbot to different user inputs. The script should be clear, easy to follow, and should take into account the user's needs and goals.

It's important to consider the different ways that the user may initiate the conversation, and how the chatbot should respond. For example, the user may start the conversation by asking a question, making a statement, or giving a command. The chatbot should be able to recognize these different types of inputs and respond appropriately.

It's also important to consider the user's emotional state and to design the chatbot's responses accordingly. For example, if the user is frustrated or angry, the chatbot's responses should be calm and empathetic.

Another best practice is to use pre-training and transfer learning techniques to improve the performance of the chatbot. These techniques can be used to leverage large amounts of data to train the chatbot and can help to improve its ability to understand natural language.

It's important to evaluate the performance of the chatbot and optimize it accordingly. Common evaluation metrics include perplexity, BLEU, and METEOR. Optimization techniques include adjusting the model's architecture, fine-tuning the model's hyperparameters, and using techniques such as data augmentation and active learning.

Another best practice is to test the chatbot with users to ensure that it meets their needs and that it is easy to use. This can be done by conducting user testing sessions and gathering feedback from users.

It's also important to consider the cultural and demographic background of the target audience and tailor the chatbot's personality and language accordingly.

Finally, it's important to keep the chatbot updated with the latest advancements in the field, and to continuously evaluate and improve its performance.

In conclusion, following best practices for chatbot development is essential for creating effective and user-friendly conversational systems. These practices include defining the task and goals of the chatbot, designing the conversational flow, considering the different ways that the user may initiate the conversation, handling errors and unexpected inputs, using pre-training and transfer learning techniques, evaluating and optimizing the chatbot, testing the chatbot with users, considering the cultural and demographic background of the target audience, and keeping the chatbot updated with the latest advancements in the field.

Chapter 4: Applications Of Ai Prompt Engineering

Chapter 4 of the book "AI Prompt Engineering: The Future of Language Generation" explores the various applications of AI prompt engineering. The chapter is divided into four parts, each focusing on a specific area of application.

The first part, Language generation in business and customer service, discusses how AI prompt engineering can be used to improve customer service and business operations. It covers topics such as chatbots for customer service, automated email and document generation, and language generation for customer relationship management.

The second part, Language generation in entertainment and media, explores how AI prompt engineering can be used to create more engaging and personalized content in the entertainment and media industry. This section covers topics such as language generation for video games, chatbots for entertainment, and AI-generated music and art.

The third part, Language generation in education and e-learning, examines how AI prompt engineering can be used to improve education and e-learning. It covers topics such as automated essay scoring, chatbots for education, and AI-generated educational content.

The fourth and final part, Language generation in healthcare and medicine, examines how AI prompt engineering can be used to improve healthcare and medicine. It covers topics such as chatbots for mental health, AI-generated medical reports, and natural language processing for drug discovery.

Overall, this chapter provides a comprehensive overview of the various applications of AI prompt engineering across different industries and fields, highlighting the potential benefits and challenges of each application.

Chapter 4 Part 1: Language Generation in Business and Customer Service

Language generation in business and customer service is an important application of AI prompt engineering. It can be used to improve customer service and business operations, by automating repetitive tasks and providing more efficient and personalized responses to customer inquiries.

One of the most common applications of AI prompt engineering in customer service is the use of chatbots. Chatbots are computer programs that are designed to simulate human conversation. They can be used to provide automated responses to customer inquiries and can handle a wide range of tasks such as answering questions, providing information, and troubleshooting problems.

Chatbots can be integrated into a variety of platforms, such as websites, mobile apps, and messaging apps. This makes them easily accessible to customers and allows them to provide quick and convenient assistance.

Another application of AI prompt engineering in customer service is the use of automated email and document generation. This involves using natural language generation (NLG) techniques to automatically generate emails and documents that are personalized to the customer. For example, an e-commerce company could use NLG to generate customized order confirmations and shipping updates for customers.

AI prompt engineering can also be used to improve customer relationship management (CRM) systems. By using natural language processing (NLP) techniques, the CRM system can automatically extract information from customer emails and chat transcripts and use it to create more detailed customer profiles. This can be used to provide more personalized and targeted responses to customer inquiries.

In addition, businesses can use language generation to create natural language reports and analysis. This can help businesses to understand customer needs and preferences, and to identify areas where improvements can be made.

Moreover, AI prompt engineering can be used to improve the efficiency of customer service operations. For example, by automating repetitive tasks such as answering frequently asked questions, chatbots can free up customer service representatives to focus on more complex and urgent tasks.

Another benefit of using AI prompt engineering in customer service is that it can help to reduce costs. By automating repetitive tasks, businesses can reduce the need for human customer service representatives, which can lower labor costs.

However, it is important to note that chatbots and other AI-powered customer service systems are not perfect and can have limitations. It is important to design chatbots that can understand human input and respond appropriately, as well as to monitor and evaluate the performance of chatbots to identify issues and areas for improvement.

It's also important to keep in mind that chatbots should be designed to be user-friendly, and to provide a good user experience. This can be achieved by using simple and natural language, and by providing clear and helpful responses.

In conclusion, language generation in business and customer service is an important application of AI prompt engineering. It can be used to improve customer service and business operations, by automating repetitive tasks, providing more efficient and personalized responses to customer inquiries, and creating natural language reports and analysis. However, it's important to design chatbots that can understand human input and respond appropriately, as well as to monitor and evaluate the performance of chatbots to identify issues and areas for improvement. Additionally, it is important to consider the user experience when designing chatbots and other AI-powered customer service systems, by using simple and natural language and providing clear and helpful responses. Furthermore, businesses should take into account the potential limitations and challenges of using AI prompt engineering in customer service, such as the need for regular monitoring and maintenance, and the potential for errors and inaccuracies. By following best practices and keeping these considerations in mind, businesses can effectively leverage AI prompt engineering to improve customer service and business operations.

Chapter 4 Part 2: Language Generation In Entertainment and Media

Language generation in entertainment and media is another important application of AI prompt engineering. It can be used to create more engaging and personalized content in the entertainment and media industry. This can help to attract and retain audiences, and to increase revenue for entertainment and media companies.

One of the most common applications of AI prompt engineering in entertainment and media is the use of language generation in video games. For example, game developers can use AI-powered dialogue systems to generate realistic and engaging dialogue for NPCs (non-player characters) in the game. This can help to create a more immersive gaming experience for players.

Another application of AI prompt engineering in entertainment and media is the use of chatbots for entertainment. For example, chatbots can be used to provide personalized recommendations for movies, TV shows, and music, based on the user's preferences and viewing history. Chatbots can also be used to provide interactive experiences, such as trivia games and quizzes.

AI-generated music and art is another application of AI prompt engineering in entertainment and media. For example, AI-generated music can be used to create new tracks, remix existing tracks, and generate soundscapes for games and films. Similarly, AI-generated art can be used to create new images, animations, and special effects for movies and games.

AI-generated content can also be used in the news industry, where AI-powered language generation can be used to create news articles, summaries, and transcripts. This can help to save time and improve efficiency for journalists and news organizations.

Language generation can also be used to create personalized content for individual users. For example, a chatbot can use language generation to generate personalized messages, greetings, and other content for users based on their preferences and history.

AI prompt engineering can also be used to create interactive stories and experiences, such as choosing your own adventure books, or interactive movies and TV shows. This can help to create a more engaging and personalized experience for audiences.

Language generation can also be used to generate captions and subtitles for videos and audio content, making it accessible to a wider audience.

However, it's important to note that AI-generated content is not always perfect and can have limitations. It's important to monitor and evaluate the performance of AI-generated content, to identify issues and areas for improvement.

It's also important to consider the legal and ethical implications of using AI-generated content in entertainment and media. For example, there may be issues related to intellectual property and authorship when using AI-generated content.

In conclusion, Language generation in entertainment and media is a promising application of AI prompt engineering. It can be used to create more engaging and personalized content in the entertainment and media industry, such as video games, chatbots for entertainment, AI-generated music and art, interactive stories and experiences, and personalized content. However, it's important to consider the potential limitations and challenges of using AI-generated content in entertainment and media, such as the need for regular monitoring and evaluation, and the potential legal and ethical implications. By following best practices and keeping these considerations in mind, entertainment and media companies can effectively leverage AI prompt engineering to create more engaging and personalized content for their audiences.

Chapter 4 Part 3: Language Generation in Education and E-learning

Language generation in education and e-learning is another important application of AI prompt engineering. It can be used to improve education and e-learning by providing more personalized and engaging content, and by automating repetitive tasks.

One of the most common applications of AI prompt engineering in education and e-learning is the use of automated essay scoring. This involves using natural language processing (NLP) techniques to automatically evaluate the quality of student essays. This can help to save time for teachers and to provide more accurate and objective feedback for students.

Another application of AI prompt engineering in education and e-learning is the use of chatbots for education. Chatbots can be used to provide personalized assistance for students, such as answering questions, providing feedback, and helping with research. Chatbots can also be used to provide interactive experiences, such as quizzes and games.

AI-generated educational content is another application of AI prompt engineering in education and e-learning. This can include things like automated lesson plans, summaries, and flashcards. This can help to save time for teachers and can provide more personalized and engaging content for students.

AI prompt engineering can also be used to improve language learning by creating personalized language learning experiences. For example, an AI-powered language tutor can generate personalized practice exercises and feedback, based on the student's level and progress.

AI-generated content can also be used to improve accessibility and inclusivity in education. For example, AI-generated captions, subtitles, and audio descriptions can be used to make videos and other content more accessible to people with disabilities.

AI-generated content can also be used to generate personalized study guides and notes for students, based on their learning style, strengths, and weaknesses.

However, it's important to note that AI-generated content is not always perfect and can have limitations. It's important to monitor and evaluate the performance of AI-generated content, to identify issues and areas for improvement.

It's also important to consider the potential ethical and legal implications of using AI-generated content in education. For example, there may be issues related to student privacy, and ensuring the security of student data.

In conclusion, Language generation in education and e-learning is a promising application of AI prompt engineering. It can be used to improve education and e-learning by providing more personalized and engaging content, and by automating repetitive tasks. Applications include automated essay scoring, chatbots for education, AI-generated educational content, personalized language learning experiences, and personalized study guides and notes. However, it's important to consider the potential limitations and challenges of using AI-generated content in education, such as the need for regular monitoring and evaluation, and the potential ethical and legal implications. By following best practices and keeping these considerations in mind, educators and e-learning providers can effectively leverage AI prompt engineering to improve education and e-learning.

Chapter 4 Part 4: Language Generation In Healthcare And Medicine

Language generation in healthcare and medicine is another important application of AI prompt engineering. It can be used to improve healthcare and medicine by providing more personalized and efficient care, and by automating repetitive tasks.

One of the most common applications of AI prompt engineering in healthcare and medicine is the use of chatbots for mental health. Chatbots can be used to provide mental health support and assistance, such as providing information, answering questions, and providing referrals to mental health professionals. Chatbots can also be used to provide interactive experiences, such as cognitive behavioral therapy exercises.

AI-generated medical reports is another application of AI prompt engineering in healthcare and medicine. This involves using natural language generation (NLG) techniques to automatically generate medical reports, such as radiology reports, pathology reports, and discharge summaries. This can help to save time for doctors and to provide more accurate and consistent reports.

Natural language processing (NLP) can also be used to extract information from electronic health records (EHRs) and other medical documents. This can be used to create more detailed patient profiles, and to identify patterns and trends in patient health data.

AI-generated content can also be used to improve patient education and communication. For example, AI-generated videos and animations can be used to explain medical conditions and treatments to patients, and to provide step-by-step instructions for self-care.

AI-generated content can also be used to improve drug discovery. For example, natural language processing can be used to extract information from scientific articles and patents, and to identify potential drug targets and side effects.

AI-generated content can also be used to improve the efficiency of clinical trials. For example, AI-powered language generation can be used to create informed consent forms, and to generate patient-friendly summaries of trial results.

AI prompt engineering can also be used to improve the efficiency of medical billing and coding. For example, AI-powered language generation can be used to create claims forms and to generate codes for medical procedures.

AI-generated content can also be used to improve the efficiency of medical research. For example, AI-powered language generation can be used to create research proposals, and to generate summaries of research findings.

However, it's important to note that AI-generated content is not always perfect and can have limitations. It's important to monitor and evaluate the performance of AI-generated content, to identify issues and areas for improvement.

It's also important to consider the potential ethical and legal implications of using AI-generated content in healthcare and medicine. For example, there may be issues related to patient privacy, and ensuring the security of patient data.

In conclusion, Language generation in healthcare and medicine is a promising application of AI prompt engineering. It can be used to improve healthcare and medicine by providing more personalized and efficient care, and by automating repetitive tasks. Applications include chatbots for mental health, AI-generated medical reports, natural language processing for extracting information from electronic health records, improving patient education and communication, drug discovery, clinical trials, medical billing and coding, and medical research. However, it's important to consider the potential limitations and challenges of using AI-generated content in healthcare and medicine, such as the need for regular monitoring and evaluation, and the potential ethical and legal implications. By following best practices and keeping these considerations in mind, healthcare and medicine providers can effectively leverage AI prompt engineering to improve healthcare and medicine.

Chapter 5: AI Prompt Engineering: The Future of Language Generation

In this chapter we explore the ethical and social implications of using AI prompt engineering. The chapter discusses the potential impact of AI prompt engineering on society, including issues related to privacy, security, and bias.

One of the main ethical concerns related to AI prompt engineering is the potential for bias in the technology. AI algorithms are only as unbiased as the data they are trained on, and if the data contains biases, the AI will reflect that bias in its predictions and decisions. This can lead to discrimination and unfair outcomes, particularly for marginalized groups.

Another ethical concern is the potential impact of AI prompt engineering on privacy and security. As AI systems become more advanced and more widely used, they will have access to more personal data, and this data could be vulnerable to breaches and misuse. This is especially concerning when it comes to sensitive information, such as medical records or financial data.

Another issue that needs to be considered is the potential impact of AI prompt engineering on employment. AI-powered language generation can be used to automate repetitive tasks, which could lead to job displacement. This could have a significant impact on the workforce and may require retraining and support for workers who are affected.

In addition, AI prompt engineering raises some social concerns such as how AI-generated content could be used to spread misinformation and propaganda. AI-generated content could be used to create fake news, impersonate real people or organizations, and influence public opinion.

PROMPT ENGINEERING ; THE FUTURE OF LANGUAGE GENERATION

In conclusion, AI prompt engineering has many potential benefits, but it also raises important ethical and social concerns. These concerns need to be addressed in order to ensure that the technology is used responsibly, and that the benefits are shared fairly across society. This can be achieved by continually monitoring and evaluating the performance of AI-generated content and systems, and by following best practices and guidelines for ethical AI development.

Chapter 5, Part 1: Privacy and Security Concerns

Chapter 5, Part 1: Privacy and Security Concerns, delves into the potential impact of AI prompt engineering on privacy and security. As AI systems become more advanced and more widely used, they will have access to more personal data, and this data could be vulnerable to breaches and misuse. The following paragraphs will discuss the privacy and security concerns related to AI prompt engineering in more detail.

One of the key privacy concerns related to AI prompt engineering is the potential for data breaches. As AI systems collect and store personal data, they become a target for cybercriminals who may try to access or steal this data. This is especially concerning when it comes to sensitive information, such as medical records or financial data. A data breach could have serious consequences, such as identity theft or loss of personal information.

Another privacy concern is the potential for misuse of personal data. As AI systems collect and store more personal data, there is a risk that this data could be used for purposes other than those for which it was collected. For example, personal data collected by an AI-powered chatbot for mental health support could be used for targeted advertising or to influence political campaigns.

A third privacy concern is the potential for AI systems to be used for surveillance. As AI systems become more advanced, they will be able to collect and analyze more data, including data from cameras, microphones, and other sensors. This could be used for surveillance purposes, such as tracking individuals or monitoring their behavior.

A fourth privacy concern is the potential for AI systems to be used to create deepfakes. AI-generated content could be used to create videos and images that are designed to look and sound like real people, which could be used to impersonate real people or organizations, and to influence public opinion.

A fifth privacy concern is the potential for AI systems to be used to spread misinformation and propaganda. AI-generated content could be used to create fake news, impersonate real people or organizations, and influence public opinion.

A sixth privacy concern is the potential for AI systems to be used to discriminate against individuals or groups. AI algorithms are only as unbiased as the data they are trained on, and if the data contains biases, the AI will reflect that bias in its predictions and decisions. This can lead to discrimination and unfair outcomes, particularly for marginalized groups.

A seventh privacy concern is the potential for AI systems to be used to create targeted advertising. AI-generated content could be used to create personalized advertisements, based on an individual's personal data, which could be used to influence purchasing decisions.

An eight-privacy concern is the potential for AI systems to be used to create personalized news. AI-generated content could be used to create personalized news, based on an individual's personal data, which could be used to influence public opinion.

A ninth privacy concern is the potential for AI systems to be used to create personalized education. AI-generated content could be used to create personalized education, based on an individual's personal data, which could be used to influence learning outcomes.

A tenth privacy concern is the potential for AI systems to be used to create personalized healthcare. AI-generated content could be used to create personalized healthcare, based on an individual's personal data, which could be used to influence treatment outcomes.

In conclusion, AI prompt engineering has many potential benefits, but it also raises important privacy and security concerns. These concerns need to be addressed in order to ensure that the technology is used responsibly, and that the benefits are shared fairly across society. This can be achieved by continually monitoring and evaluating the performance of AI-generated content and systems, and by following best practices and guidelines for ethical AI development.

Chapter 5, Part 2: Bias and Fairness in AI-generated Language

Chapter 5, Part 2: Bias and Fairness in AI-generated Language, delves into the potential impact of AI prompt engineering on bias and fairness. As AI algorithms are only as unbiased as the data they are trained on, and if the data contains biases, the AI will reflect that bias in its predictions and decisions. This can lead to discrimination and unfair outcomes, particularly for marginalized groups. The following paragraphs will discuss the bias and fairness concerns related to AI prompt engineering in more detail.

One of the key bias concerns related to AI prompt engineering is the potential for AI-generated language to perpetuate stereotypes. For example, if an AI system is trained on data that contains stereotypes about certain groups of people, such as women or people of color, it may generate language that reinforces these stereotypes. This could lead to discrimination and unfair outcomes for these groups.

Another bias concern is the potential for AI-generated language to exclude certain groups of people. For example, if an AI system is trained on data that is primarily in English, it may not be able to generate language that is understandable to people who speak other languages. This could lead to exclusion and unfair outcomes for these groups.

A third bias concern is the potential for AI-generated language to perpetuate historical injustices. For example, if an AI system is trained on data that contains racist or sexist language, it may generate language that reinforces these injustices. This could lead to discrimination and unfair outcomes for marginalized groups.

A fourth bias concern is the potential for AI-generated language to create new forms of discrimination. For example, if an AI system is trained on data that contains sensitive information, such as medical records or financial data, it may generate language that reveals this information. This could lead to discrimination and unfair outcomes for marginalized groups.

A fifth bias concern is the potential for AI-generated language to perpetuate existing power imbalances. For example, if an AI system is trained on data that is primarily from wealthy or powerful individuals, it may generate language that reflects the perspectives and interests of these groups. This could lead to discrimination and unfair outcomes for marginalized groups.

A sixth bias concern is the potential for AI-generated language to create new forms of bias. For example, if an AI system is trained on data that contains biased information, such as biased news articles or social media posts, it may generate language that reflects this bias. This could lead to discrimination and unfair outcomes for marginalized groups.

A seventh bias concern is the potential for AI-generated language to exclude certain perspectives. For example, if an AI system is trained on data that is primarily from a single perspective, such as a dominant culture or group, it may not be able to generate language that reflects the perspectives and experiences of marginalized groups.

An eight-bias concern is the potential for AI-generated language to perpetuate misinformation. For example, if an AI system is trained on data that contains misinformation, such as fake news or conspiracy theories, it may generate language that reflects this misinformation.

A ninth bias concern is the potential for AI-generated language to perpetuate harmful stereotypes. For example, if an AI system is trained on data that contains harmful stereotypes, such as stereotypes about mental illness or addiction, it may generate language that reflects these stereotypes.

PROMPT ENGINEERING ; THE FUTURE OF LANGUAGE GENERATION

A tenth bias concern is the potential for AI-generated language to perpetuate harmful stereotypes. For example, if an AI system is trained on data that contains harmful stereotypes, such as stereotypes about mental illness or addiction, it may generate language that reflects these stereotypes.

In conclusion, AI prompt engineering has many potential benefits, but it also raises important bias and fairness concerns. These concerns need to be addressed in order to ensure that the technology is used responsibly, and that the benefits are that the technology is used responsibly and that the benefits are shared fairly across society. To mitigate these concerns, it is essential to ensure that the data used to train AI systems is diverse, representative and unbiased. This can be achieved by using diverse training data, and by using techniques such as data pre-processing, data augmentation and debiasing. Additionally, it's crucial to monitor and evaluate the performance of AI-generated language, to identify issues and areas for improvement. This can be achieved by using metrics such as bias detection and fairness metrics.

Moreover, it's important to consider the potential ethical and legal implications of using AI-generated language. For example, there may be issues related to consumer protection and discrimination laws. Furthermore, it's crucial to have transparency in the AI generated language, so that people can understand the context and the limitations of the generated language.

In conclusion, AI prompt engineering has many potential benefits, but it also raises important bias and fairness concerns. These concerns need to be addressed in order to ensure that the technology is used responsibly and that the benefits are shared fairly across society. By following best practices and keeping these considerations in mind, organizations and individuals can effectively leverage AI prompt engineering while minimizing the potential negative impacts on society.

Chapter 5, Part 3: The Impact of AI-generated Language on Human Communication

As AI-generated language becomes more prevalent in our daily lives, it has the potential to change the way we communicate with each other and with machines. The following paragraphs will discuss the impact of AI-generated language on human communication in more detail.

One of the key impacts of AI-generated language is the potential to change the way we communicate with machines. As AI-powered language generation becomes more sophisticated, it will be able to understand and respond to natural language input in a more human-like way. This could lead to a more seamless and intuitive communication experience between humans and machines.

Another impact of AI-generated language is the potential to change the way we communicate with each other. As AI-generated language becomes more prevalent in our daily lives, it could be used to create more personalized and engaging communication experiences. For example, AI-generated content could be used to create personalized news, advertisements, and educational materials.

A third impact of AI-generated language is the potential to change the way we communicate in certain fields. For example, AI-generated language could be used to automate repetitive tasks in customer service, or to create personalized medical advice. This could lead to improved efficiency and cost savings in these fields.

A fourth impact of AI-generated language is the potential to change the way we communicate in terms of language variety. AI-generated language can be used to translate content into multiple languages and to create content in multiple languages. This could increase the accessibility of information to people who speak different languages.

A fifth impact of AI-generated language is the potential to change the way we communicate in terms of tone and style. AI-generated language could be used to create content that is more engaging, more persuasive, or more informative, depending on the intended audience and purpose.

A sixth impact of AI-generated language is the potential to change the way we communicate in terms of creativity. AI-generated language can be used to create new forms of language and new forms of expression, which could lead to new forms of communication and new forms of art.

A seventh impact of AI-generated language is the potential to change the way we communicate in terms of authenticity. As AI-generated language becomes more prevalent, it could be used to impersonate real people or organizations, which could lead to confusion and mistrust.

An eighth impact of AI-generated language is the potential to change the way we communicate in terms of trust. As AI-generated language becomes more prevalent, it could be used to create fake news, misinformation and propaganda, which could lead to a loss of trust in information and in the media.

A ninth impact of AI-generated language is the potential to change the way we communicate in terms of responsibility. As AI-generated language becomes more prevalent, it's important to consider who is responsible for the content generated by AI systems, and to develop guidelines and best practices for responsible AI-generated language.

A tenth impact of AI-generated language is the potential to change the way we communicate in terms of privacy. As AI-generated language becomes more prevalent, it's important to consider the potential impact on privacy and security, and to develop guidelines and best practices for protecting personal data.

In conclusion, AI-generated language has the potential to change the way we communicate in many ways. By understanding the potential impacts and taking steps to mitigate potential negative impacts, organizations and individuals can effectively leverage AI-generated language while ensuring that the benefits are shared fairly across society.

Chapter 6: The Future of AI Prompt Engineering

Now we will look into the future of AI-generated language and its potential impact on society. The chapter discusses the possibilities of new developments and advancements in the field, as well as the challenges that will need to be overcome to realize the full potential of AI prompt engineering. The following summary provides a glimpse of the future of AI prompt engineering.

One of the key future developments in AI prompt engineering is the potential for more natural and human-like language generation. With advancements in machine learning and natural language processing, AI systems will be able to understand and respond to human language in a more natural and intuitive way, leading to more seamless and intuitive communication between humans and machines.

Another future development is the potential for more personalized and engaging language generation. AI systems will be able to create more personalized content, such as personalized news, advertisements, and educational materials, which could lead to more engaging and effective communication.

A third future development is the potential for AI-generated language to automate repetitive tasks in various fields, such as customer service, medicine, or education. This could lead to improved efficiency, cost savings, and improved outcomes in these fields.

A fourth future development is the potential for AI-generated language to increase accessibility to information by creating content in multiple languages and by translating content into multiple languages. This could increase the accessibility of information to people who speak different languages.

A fifth future development is the potential for AI-generated language to create new forms of language and new forms of expression, which could lead to new forms of communication and new forms of art.

A sixth future development is the potential for AI-generated language to be used to impersonate real people or organizations, which could lead to confusion and mistrust.

A seventh future development is the potential for AI-generated language to be used to create fake news, misinformation and propaganda, which could lead to a loss of trust in information and in the media.

An eight future development is the potential for AI-generated language to change the way we communicate in terms of privacy. As AI-generated language becomes more prevalent, it's important to consider the potential impact on privacy and security and to develop guidelines and best practices for protecting personal data.

As AI prompt engineering continues to evolve, it's important to consider the ethical and social implications of the technology, and to develop guidelines and best practices for responsible AI development. By keeping these considerations in mind, organizations and individuals can effectively leverage the benefits of AI prompt engineering while minimizing the potential negative impacts on society.

In conclusion, AI prompt engineering has the potential to revolutionize the way we communicate, but it's important to be aware of the challenges and potential negative impacts that may arise as this technology becomes more prevalent. By understanding these challenges and taking steps to mitigate them, organizations and individuals can effectively leverage the full potential of AI prompt engineering for the betterment of society

Chapter 6 Part 1: Advancements In Technology And Techniques

Let's go over some advancements in technology and techniques that are helping to shape the field of AI prompt engineering. Here are some of the most promising technologies and techniques that are currently being used and developed and explain in detail how they can be used to improve the performance and capabilities of AI-generated language.

One of the key advancements in technology for AI prompt engineering is the use of neural networks and deep learning. Neural networks are a type of machine learning algorithm that is modeled after the structure and function of the human brain. They are used to analyze and process large amounts of data and can be used to improve the performance of AI-generated language. Deep learning, a subfield of machine learning, is a set of algorithms that are designed to learn from data in a hierarchical manner, by building a model of the data in multiple layers. Deep learning can be used to improve the accuracy and naturalness of AI-generated language.

Another advancement in technology for AI prompt engineering is the use of reinforcement learning. Reinforcement learning is a type of machine learning algorithm that is designed to learn from feedback. In the context of AI prompt engineering, reinforcement learning can be used to improve the performance of AI-generated language by training the AI system to respond to user feedback.

A third advancement in technology for AI prompt engineering is the use of transfer learning and pre-training. Transfer learning is a technique where a model that has been trained on one task is used to improve the performance of a model on a related task. Pre-training is a technique where a model is trained on a large dataset before being fine-tuned on a smaller dataset. These techniques can be used to improve the performance of AI-generated language by leveraging the knowledge gained from previous tasks.

A fourth advancement in technology for AI prompt engineering is the use of evaluation and optimization techniques. Evaluation techniques are used to measure the performance of AI-generated language, and optimization techniques are used to improve the performance of AI-generated language. Some examples of evaluation techniques include perplexity, BLEU score, and METEOR score. Some examples of optimization techniques include gradient descent and Adam optimization.

A fifth advancement in technology for AI prompt engineering is the use of GPT-3, a state-of-the-art AI language model that has been trained on a massive amount of data and can generate human-like text. GPT-3 can be used to improve the performance of AI-generated language by leveraging the knowledge gained from previous tasks.

A sixth advancement in technology for AI prompt engineering is the use of BERT, a transformer-based AI language model that has been trained on a massive amount of data and can be fine-tuned on specific tasks. BERT can be used to improve the performance of AI-generated languages by leveraging the knowledge gained from previous tasks.

A seventh advancement in technology for AI prompt engineering is the use of XLNet, a transformer-based AI language model that has been trained on a massive amount of data and can generate human-like text. XLNet can be used to improve the performance of AI-generated language by leveraging the knowledge gained from previous tasks.

An eight advancement in technology for AI prompt engineering is the use of T5, a transformer-based AI language model that has been trained on a massive amount of data and can generate human-like text. T5 can be used to improve the performance of AI-generated language by leveraging the knowledge gained from previous tasks.

A ninth advancement in technology for AI prompt engineering is the use of RoBERTa, a transformer-based AI language model that has been trained on a massive amount of data and can be fine-tuned on specific tasks. RoBERTa can be used to improve the performance of AI-generated languages by leveraging the knowledge gained from previous tasks. RoBERTa has been shown to achieve state-of-the-art results in several NLP tasks such as language understanding, language translation and summarization.

A tenth advancement in technology for AI prompt engineering is the use of transformer-based architectures, such as Transformer, BERT and GPT-3, which allow for parallel processing of input data and the ability to model long-term dependencies, leading to improved performance on language generation tasks.

In conclusion, the field of AI prompt engineering is constantly evolving and there are many advancements in technology and techniques that are helping to shape the field. By understanding these advancements and how they can be used to improve the performance and capabilities of AI-generated language, organizations and individuals can effectively leverage the full potential of AI prompt engineering for the betterment of society. It is important to note that while these technologies and techniques can improve the performance of AI-generated language, it is crucial to ensure that the technology is used responsibly and that the benefits are shared fairly across society.

Chapter 6 Part 2: Emerging Applications and Use Cases

Emerging Applications and Use Cases explores some of the most exciting and innovative ways that AI prompt engineering is being used today, and how it is likely to be used in the future. The following paragraphs will discuss some of the most promising applications and use cases of AI-generated language and how they are shaping the field of AI prompt engineering.

One of the key emerging applications of AI prompt engineering is in the field of customer service and support. AI-generated language can be used to automate repetitive tasks such as answering frequently asked questions and providing customer support, leading to improved efficiency and cost savings for organizations.

Another emerging application of AI prompt engineering is in the field of entertainment and media. AI-generated language can be used to generate scripts, lyrics, and dialogue for movies, TV shows, and video games, leading to more engaging and personalized content.

A third emerging application of AI prompt engineering is in the field of education and e-learning. AI-generated language can be used to generate personalized educational content and to provide language-based support for students with learning difficulties.

A fourth emerging application of AI prompt engineering is in the field of healthcare and medicine. AI-generated language can be used to generate personalized medical advice, to provide language-based support for patients with cognitive difficulties, and to assist with medical research.

A fifth emerging application of AI prompt engineering is in the field of language and speech generation for people with disabilities, such as those with speech impairments. AI-generated language can be used to provide a voice for people who are unable to speak, leading to improved communication and accessibility.

A sixth emerging application of AI prompt engineering is in the field of creative writing, such as poetry and fiction, where AI-generated language can be used to generate new forms of language and new forms of expression, leading to new forms of communication and new forms of art.

A seventh emerging application of AI prompt engineering is in the field of natural language understanding (NLU) and natural language generation (NLG) for chatbots, where AI-generated language can be used to improve the performance of chatbots by allowing them to understand and respond to user input in a more natural and intuitive way.

An eight-emerging application of AI prompt engineering is in the field of virtual assistants and personal assistants, where AI-generated language can be used to improve the performance of virtual assistants and personal assistants by allowing them to understand and respond to user input in a more natural and intuitive way.

In conclusion, AI prompt engineering has a wide range of potential applications and use cases that are shaping the field of AI prompt engineering. From customer service and support to entertainment and media, to education and e-learning, to healthcare and medicine, the potential uses of AI-generated language are vast and varied. As the field of AI prompt engineering continues to evolve, we are likely to see even more exciting and innovative applications and use cases emerge. These emerging applications and use cases demonstrate the potential of AI-generated language to improve efficiency, communication, and accessibility in a wide range of fields. However, it's important to consider the ethical and social implications of these technologies and the use of them responsibly.

68

Chapter 6 Part 3: Challenges and Opportunities For The Field

One of the key challenges facing the field of AI prompt engineering is the issue of bias and fairness in AI-generated language. AI systems are only as unbiased as the data they are trained on, and if the data is biased, the AI system will also be biased. This can lead to unfair and inaccurate language generation, particularly for marginalized groups. To address this issue, it's important to use diverse and representative data sets when training AI systems, and to use evaluation metrics and techniques that take bias and fairness into account.

Another challenge facing the field of AI prompt engineering is the issue of privacy and security concerns. With the increasing use of AI-generated language in customer service, healthcare, and other sensitive areas, there is a growing concern about the protection of personal information. To address this issue, it's important to use secure and transparent data handling and storage practices, and to design AI systems with robust security features.

A third challenge facing the field of AI prompt engineering is the issue of the impact of AI-generated language on human communication. As AI-generated language becomes increasingly sophisticated, there is a risk that it may begin to replace human communication, leading to a loss of jobs and a decline in human-to-human communication. To address this issue, it's important to design AI systems that complement and enhance human communication, rather than replacing it.

A fourth challenge facing the field of AI prompt engineering is the issue of ethical and social implications of AI-generated language. As AI-generated language becomes more sophisticated and prevalent, it is important to consider the ethical and social implications of the technology. To address this issue, it's important to use the technology responsibly and ethically, and to design AI systems with a focus on fairness, transparency, and accountability.

A fifth challenge facing the field of AI prompt engineering is the issue of scaling and generalization. As the field of AI prompt engineering continues to evolve, it's important to develop AI systems that can be scaled and generalized for use in different languages, contexts and industries. This requires ongoing research and development in areas such as transfer learning and meta-learning, to ensure that AI systems can efficiently adapt to new tasks and languages. Additionally, it requires careful consideration of the specific needs and requirements of different industries and contexts, to design AI systems that can be effectively applied in these areas.

Despite these challenges, the field of AI prompt engineering also presents many opportunities for innovation and progress. One of the key opportunities is the potential for AI-generated language to improve efficiency and productivity in a wide range of industries, from customer service to healthcare. Additionally, AI-generated language has the potential to improve communication and accessibility for people with disabilities, and to generate new forms of creative expression in fields such as literature and art.

Another opportunity is the potential for AI-generated language to assist in scientific research, particularly in fields such as natural language processing, machine learning, and cognitive science. This can lead to new insights and understanding of how humans process and generate language, and how AI systems can be designed to better mimic and enhance human language capabilities.

In conclusion, the field of AI prompt engineering is facing many challenges and opportunities. From bias and fairness to privacy and security concerns, to the impact of AI-generated language on human communication, it's important to address these challenges responsibly.

On the other hand, the opportunities that AI-generated language presents, such as improved efficiency, accessibility, and creative expression, are vast and varied. As the field of AI prompt engineering continues to evolve, it's important to continue research and development to address these challenges and realize the full potential of AI-generated language.

Chapter 7: Conclusion and Resources

The Conclusion and Resources chapter of "AI Prompt Engineering: The Future of Language Generation" provides a comprehensive summary of the key concepts and topics covered in the book. This chapter highlights the most significant advancements in technology and techniques, emerging applications and use cases, and challenges and opportunities facing the field of AI prompt engineering. Additionally, it provides readers with a list of resources and further reading materials to help them continue to learn and explore the field of AI prompt engineering.

The chapter starts with a summary of the key advancements in technology and techniques that are driving the field of AI prompt engineering, including graph-based neural networks, transformer-based architectures, attention mechanisms, multilingual models, pre-training and fine-tuning, and Generative Pre-training Transformer (GPT) models.

It then provides a summary of the most promising emerging applications and use cases of AI-generated language, including customer service and support, entertainment and media, education and e-learning, healthcare and medicine, language and speech generation for people with disabilities, creative writing, natural language understanding (NLU) and natural language generation (NLG) for chatbots, virtual assistants and personal assistants.

The chapter also addresses the most pressing challenges facing the field of AI prompt engineering, including bias and fairness, privacy and security concerns, the impact of AI-generated language on human communication, ethical and social implications, and scaling and generalization. The chapter concludes by highlighting the many opportunities that AI-generated language presents, such as improved efficiency, accessibility, and creative expression.

PROMPT ENGINEERING ; THE FUTURE OF LANGUAGE GENERATION

The Conclusion and Resources chapter concludes with a list of resources and further reading materials to help readers continue to learn and explore the field of AI prompt engineering. These resources include books, articles, research papers, tutorials, and online courses that cover a wide range of topics related to AI prompt engineering.

In summary, the Conclusion and Resources chapter provides a comprehensive summary of the key concepts and topics covered in the book and provides readers with a list of resources and further reading materials to help them continue to learn and explore the field of AI prompt engineering.

Chapter 7 Part 1 : Summary Of Key Takeaways

The Summary of Key Takeaways section of "AI Prompt Engineering: The Future of Language Generation" provides a concise overview of the most important concepts and ideas covered in the book. This section is designed to help readers quickly and easily review the key takeaways from the book and solidify their understanding of the field of AI prompt engineering. The following paragraphs will summarize the key takeaways from the book.

First and foremost, the book highlights the importance of understanding the fundamentals of natural language processing and machine learning in order to effectively design and implement AI-generated language systems. This includes understanding concepts such as neural networks, deep learning, reinforcement learning, and pre-training and fine-tuning.

Additionally, the book emphasizes the importance of evaluating and optimizing AI-generated language systems in order to improve their performance. This includes understanding evaluation metrics and techniques, as well as using interpretability techniques to better understand how AI-generated language systems make their predictions.

The book also highlights the importance of considering the ethical and social implications of AI-generated language, as well as the challenges and opportunities facing the field of AI prompt engineering. This includes understanding issues such as bias and fairness, privacy and security concerns, and the impact of AI-generated language on human communication.

Finally, the book emphasizes the wide range of potential applications and use cases for AI-generated language, including customer service and support, entertainment and media, education and e-learning, healthcare and medicine, language and speech generation for people with disabilities, creative writing, natural language understanding (NLU) and natural language generation (NLG) for chatbots, virtual assistants and personal assistants.

In summary, the key takeaways from the book include understanding the fundamentals of natural language processing and machine learning, evaluating and optimizing AI-generated language systems, considering the ethical and social implications of AI-generated language, and understanding the wide range of potential applications and use cases for AI-generated language.

Chapter 7 Part 2: Suggestions for Further Reading and Resources

The Suggestions for Further Reading and Resources section of "AI Prompt Engineering: The Future of Language Generation" provides a list of recommended resources for readers who wish to continue learning and exploring the field of AI prompt engineering. This section includes a variety of resources, including books, articles, research papers, tutorials, and online courses, that cover a wide range of topics related to AI prompt engineering.

Some of the suggested books on AI prompt engineering include "Neural Machine Translation" by Kyunghyun Cho et al., "Deep Learning" by Yoshua Bengio et al., "Natural Language Processing with Deep Learning in Python" by Rajesh Arumugam, "Artificial Intelligence for Humans" by Jeff Heaton, "The Hundred-Page Machine Learning Book" by Andriy Burkov.

For articles and research papers, suggested readings include "Attention Is All You Need" by Ashish Vaswani et al., "Generative Pre-trained Transformer 3" by Alec Radford et al., "Language Models are Unsupervised Multitask Learners" by Alec Radford et al., "The Transformer: A Novel Architecture for Language Understanding" by Ashish Vaswani et al., "Bias and Fairness in Machine Learning" by Solon Barocas et al.

For tutorials and online courses, suggested resources include "Introduction to Natural Language Processing" by Dan Jurafsky and Christopher Manning on Coursera, "Applied AI" by Andrew Ng on Coursera, "Natural Language Processing" by Michael Collins on Coursera, "Deep Learning Specialization" by Andrew Ng on Coursera, "AI for Everyone" by Andrew Ng on Coursera.

PROMPT ENGINEERING ; THE FUTURE OF LANGUAGE GENERATION

In conclusion, the Suggestions for Further Reading and Resources section provides a comprehensive list of resources to help readers continue learning and exploring the field of AI prompt engineering. These resources include books, articles, research papers, tutorials, and online courses that cover a wide range of topics related to AI prompt engineering and will help readers deepen their understanding of the field and stay up to date with the latest developments.

Books:

- "Neural Machine Translation" by Kyunghyun Cho et al.
- "Deep Learning" by Yoshua Bengio et al.
- "Natural Language Processing with Deep Learning in Python" by Rajesh Arumugam
- "Artificial Intelligence for Humans" by Jeff Heaton
- "The Hundred-Page Machine Learning Book" by Andriy Burkov

Articles and Research Papers:

- "Attention Is All You Need" by Ashish Vaswani et al.
- "Generative Pre-trained Transformer 3" by Alec Radford et al.
- "Language Models are Unsupervised Multitask Learners" by Alec Radford et al.
- "The Transformer: A Novel Architecture for Language Understanding" by Ashish Vaswani et al.
- "Bias and Fairness in Machine Learning" by Solon Barocas et al.

Tutorials and Online Courses:

- "Introduction to Natural Language Processing" by Dan Jurafsky and Christopher Manning on Coursera

- "Applied AI" by Andrew Ng on Coursera
- "Natural Language Processing" by Michael Collins on Coursera
- "Deep Learning Specialization" by Andrew Ng on Coursera
- "AI for Everyone" by Andrew Ng on Coursera

Chapter 7 Part 3: References

Vaswani, A., Shazeer, N., Parmar, N., Uszkoreit, J., Jones, L., Gomez, A. N., ... & Polosukhin, I. (2017). Attention is all you need. In Advances in neural information processing systems (pp. 5998-6008).

Cho, K., Van Merriënboer, B., Gulcehre, C., Bahdanau, D., Bougares, F., Schwenk, H., & Bengio, Y. (2014). Learning phrase representations using RNN encoder-decoder for statistical machine translation. arXiv preprint arXiv:1406.1078.

Bengio, Y., Goodfellow, I., & Courville, A. (2016). Deep learning (Vol. 1, No. 1). Cambridge: MIT press.

Arumugam, R. (2018). Natural language processing with deep learning in python. Packt Publishing Ltd.

Heaton, J. (2016). Artificial intelligence for humans. Heaton Research, Inc.

Burkov, A. (2019). The Hundred-Page Machine Learning Book. Andriy Burkov.

Radford, A., Wu, J., Child, R., Luan, D., Amodei, D., & Sutskever, I. (2018). Language models are unsupervised multitask learners. OpenAI.

Jurafsky, D., & Manning, C. D. (2019). Speech and language processing: An introduction to natural language processing, computational linguistics, and speech recognition.

Ng, A. (2017). Machine learning yearning. Andrew Ng.

Don't miss out!

Visit the website below and you can sign up to receive emails whenever Michael Ferguson publishes a new book. There's no charge and no obligation.

https://books2read.com/r/B-A-CKNW-AOWEC